T0113348

MEETING
JESUS

13 Studies for Individuals or Groups

J A M E S   W.   S I R E

Harold Shaw Publishers • Wheaton, Illinois

ISBN-13: 978-0-877-88542-9

146502721

CONTENTS

INTRODUCTION

Jesus is an amazingly attractive, utterly exasperating person with whom everyone should come to terms. That is the premise of these studies. I have chosen passages from the Gospels to highlight Jesus' character, especially in his confrontation with his contemporaries. As in Israel during the time of Christ, so now: Jesus comes to us in the Gospels, demanding of us what he demanded of his early disciples and would-be followers.

TAKING JESUS SERIOUSLY

But why should we take Jesus seriously? Is he not just one of many religious teachers? Why should we pay any attention to him? The answer is clear: he made some startling claims. If they are true, they apply to us as much as to his first disciples. If we are to be honest in our search for truth, we have to take him seriously.

You see, Jesus claimed to have a special insight into who God is. He claimed to act in God's place, forgiving sins and casting out demons—to be so related to God that he could call him "Daddy," something no good contemporary of his would ever do. He even thought of himself as the suffering servant of Isaiah 53, the one who would himself be the sacrifice for our sins. He insisted that what he said is so true and so important that our very lives—now and in eternity—are at stake. If we miss him, Jesus said, we miss life itself.

To modern ears—and to ancient ones, too—this sounds like madness. Surely a person who makes such radical claims is either a liar or a lunatic. So we reason, and so did his contemporaries. The choice has always been stark: liar, lunatic, or Lord. How then do we decide?

Jesus is his own best case for who he is. So "come and see" is the best single approach for a seeker to take (John 1:39, 46). That is what these studies are designed to do—help us "come and see" who this Jesus is.

HOW TO USE THIS STUDYGUIDE

Fisherman studyguides are based on the inductive approach to Bible study. Inductive study is discovery study; we discover what the Bible says as we ask questions about its content and search for answers. This is quite different from the process in which a teacher *tells* a group *about* the Bible and what it means and what to do about it. In inductive study God speaks directly to each of us through his Word.

A group functions best when a leader keeps the discussion on target, but this leader is neither the teacher nor the "answer person." A leader's responsibility is to *ask*—not *tell*. The answers come from the text itself as group members examine, discuss, and think together about the passage.

There are four kinds of questions in each study. The first is an *approach question*. Used before the Bible passage is read, this question breaks the ice and helps you focus on the topic of the Bible study. It begins to reveal where thoughts and feelings need to be transformed by Scripture.

Some of the earlier questions in each study are *observation questions* designed to help you find out basic facts—who, what, where, when, and how.

When you know what the Bible says you need to ask, *What does it mean?* These *interpretation questions* help you to discover the writer's basic message.

Application questions ask, *What does it mean to me?* They challenge you to live out the Scripture's life-transforming message.

Fisherman studyguides provide spaces between questions for jotting down responses and related questions you would like to raise in the group. Each group member should have a copy of the studyguide and may take a turn in leading the group.

A group should use any accurate, modern translation of the Bible such as the *New International Version,* the *New American Standard Bible,* the *Revised Standard Version,* the *New Jerusalem Bible,* or the *Good News Bible.* (Other translations or paraphrases of the Bible may be referred to when additional help is needed.) Bible commentaries should not be brought to a Bible study because they tend to dampen discussion and keep people from thinking for themselves.

SUGGESTIONS FOR GROUP LEADERS

1. Read and study the Bible passage thoroughly beforehand, grasping its themes and applying its teachings for yourself. Pray that the Holy Spirit will "guide you into truth" so that your leadership will guide others.

2. If the studyguide's questions ever seem ambiguous or unnatural to you, rephrase them, feeling free to add others that seem necessary to bring out the meaning of a verse.

3. Begin (and end) the study promptly. Start by asking someone to pray for God's help. Remember, the Holy Spirit is the teacher, not you!

4. Ask for volunteers to read the passages out loud.

5. As you ask the studyguide's questions in sequence, encourage everyone to participate in the discussion. If some are silent, ask, "What do you think, Heather?" or, "Dan, what can you add to that answer?" or suggest, "Let's have an answer from someone who hasn't spoken up yet."

6. If a question comes up that you can't answer, don't be afraid to admit that you're baffled! Assign the topic as a research project for someone to report on next week.

7. Keep the discussion moving and focused. Though tangents will inevitably be introduced, you can bring the discussion back to the topic at hand. Learn to pace the discussion so that you finish a study each session you meet.

8. Don't be afraid of silences: some questions take time to answer and some people need time to gather courage to speak. If silence persists, rephrase your question, but resist the temptation to answer it yourself.

9. If someone comes up with an answer that is clearly illogical or unbiblical, ask him or her for further clarification: "What verse suggests that to you?"

10. Discourage Bible-hopping and overuse of cross-references. Learn all you can from *this* passage, along with a few important references suggested in the studyguide.

11. Some questions are marked with a ♦. This indicates that further information is available in the Leader's Notes at the back of the guide.

12. For further information on getting a new Bible study group started and keeping it functioning effectively, read Gladys Hunt's *You Can Start a Bible Study Group* and *Pilgrims in Progress: Growing through Groups* by Jim and Carol Plueddemann.

SUGGESTIONS FOR GROUP MEMBERS

1. Learn and apply the following ground rules for effective Bible study. (If new members join the group later, review these guidelines with the whole group.)

2. Remember that your goal is to learn all that you can *from the Bible passage being studied.* Let it speak for itself without using Bible commentaries or other Bible passages. There is more than enough in each assigned passage to keep your group productively occupied for one session. Sticking to the passage saves the group from insecurity and confusion.

3. Avoid the temptation to bring up those fascinating tangents that don't really grow out of the passage you are discussing. If the topic is of common interest, you can bring it up later in informal conversation following the study. Meanwhile, help each other stick to the subject!

4. Encourage each other to participate. People remember best what they discover and verbalize for themselves. Some people are naturally shyer than others, or they may be afraid of making a mistake. If your discussion is free and friendly and you show real interest in what other group members think and feel, they will be more likely to speak up. Remember, the more people involved in a discussion, the richer it will be.

5. Guard yourself from answering too many questions or talking too much. Give others a chance to express themselves. If you are one who participates easily, discipline yourself by counting to ten before you open your mouth!

6. Make personal, honest applications and commit yourself to letting God's Word change you.

ENTER JESUS

Mark 1:1-34

Victor Hugo wrote in *Les Miserables,* "A cannon ball makes only two thousand miles an hour; light makes two hundred thousand miles a second. Such is the superiority of Jesus Christ over Napoleon."

Mark swiftly introduces his readers to Jesus. By the twenty-eighth verse, Jesus is locally famous. You see, he's been doing things that amaze people—and things that confuse people—because they have never seen such authority. Mark's perspective gives us a sweeping scope of the events leading to Jesus' popularity. As you study, see for yourself whether you agree with Hugo.

♦ **1.** If you were to begin to tell what you know of the story of Jesus, where would you begin? Why?

♦ *Indicates further information in Leader's Notes*

Read Mark 1:1-34.

Biblical scholars generally believe that when Jesus says, "The time has come. The kingdom of God is near. Repent and believe the good news!" (verse 15), he is summarizing his entire message.

The following questions examine instances in which the kingdom of God drew near in the world of Jesus' day.

♦ **2.** What does Mark take to be "the beginning of the gospel about Jesus Christ" (verse 1)? Why do you suppose Mark begins with a quotation from the Old Testament and then brings in John the Baptist? How does this set Jesus' life and ministry in perspective?

♦ **3.** Verses 2-3 contain a prophecy from the ancient prophet Isaiah. How does John the Baptist fulfill this Old Testament prophecy? For whom is he preparing the way?

♦ **4.** How are God the Father and God the Holy Spirit shown to be present in the beginning of Jesus' ministry (verses 9-12)?

♦ **5.** What opposing kingdom does Jesus immediately face in verses 12-13?

♦ **6.** What evidences of Jesus' authority do you see in the following verses?

Verses 16-20

Verses 21-28

Verses 29-34

♦ **7.** Mark identifies Jesus through various titles. What are they (verses 1, 3, 11, 24)? What significance do you think they have in Mark's mind?

8. What reaction do each of the following people (or sets of people) have to Jesus:

John the Baptist (verse 7)

His disciples (verses 14-20)

The people at Capernaum (verses 22, 27)

The evil spirit (verse 24)

♦ **9.** This is, of course, the first study, and much will come after it. Still, take stock of your own reaction so far. What do you think of the Jesus who emerges in this opening to Mark's account?

JESUS VISITS NAZARETH

Luke 4:14-30

Imagine Hank, your neighbor's boy. He grows up, works in his family's grocery store, then leaves to study in college. A few weeks later he returns for a weekend, and his parents invite the neighbors to a backyard party to welcome him home. You are pleased to see him and are impressed at first with his increased sophistication. But when he begins to tell you what he's learned, you gradually realize that he has been educated beyond the limits of his ego. You leave the party early, disgusted with his arrogance.

After a brief comment on Jesus' return from the desert, where he was tempted, Luke begins his story of Jesus' ministry with a trip back to his home town, Nazareth. Luke 4 captures Jesus' understanding of his mission and message. What makes the setting of this understanding so interesting is the response of his neighbors.

♦ **1.** Have you ever been away from home for a while and then returned, say after a few months at college? What sort of response did your family and friends have to the changes in your demeanor, your ideas, your possibly

changed self-understanding? Did you feel any awkwardness? Or suspicion? Or rejection? Why?

Read Luke 4:14-30.

♦ **2.** What is the initial response to Jesus' ministry (verses
15, 22)? After Jesus' elaboration and further explanation,
what is the response of his neighbors?

♦ **3.** Jesus' contemporaries held Isaiah (and Elijah and
Elisha, too) in the highest regard. When Jesus read from
Isaiah 61:1-2 and applied the description of Isaiah's own
mission to himself, how did they feel? What surprised
them?

♦ **4.** In quoting from Isaiah, whom did Jesus take to be his audience? What was his "message," that is, his agenda? Why might that upset his neighbors?

5. Instead of explaining himself when his neighbors were puzzled, Jesus suggested that their reaction could have been predicted. How would this add fuel to their fire?

♦ **6.** Why do the stories Jesus tells of Elijah and Elisha stir their anger even further?

♦ **7.** Jesus quietly escapes from the unruly mob (verse 30). What does this show us about his control of the situation? In light of who he is claiming to be, is it out of character?

♦ **8.** In responding to Jesus, what choice did his neighbors have? To what extent do you think their reaction is justified?

♦ **9.** Why do you suppose Jesus made it so hard for his neighbors to accept him and his message? What was he trying to elicit from his hometown friends?

♦ **10.** In reacting to the Jesus we see in this passage, what choices do we have today? Is the challenge to us as troublesome? Why?

JESUS FORGIVES SINS

Luke 5:17-26

Queen Elizabeth I once said to the Countess of Nottingham, who had hurt her, "God may forgive you, but I never can." Do you think the countess really felt at all forgiven, even though she'd asked God to forgive her? Since she'd offended the queen and the royal heart was against her, it's likely she spent much of her life feeling guilty.

Still, there may be hope for the Countess of Nottingham. You see, the Jews believed that *every* sin was done against God, who is perfect. So, in the record of things, God is the only one who can forgive someone for all the wrong things he or she has done. In this study we get a surprising insight on forgiveness.

◆　**1.** Think back to a time when someone offended you. What needed to happen before a good relationship between the two of you could be restored? Could anyone other than you forgive the person who offended you?

Read Luke 5:17-26.

◆ **2.** Describe the scene in this passage: How large a cross-section of people is there? Where are they? What was Jesus doing before the interruption? What kind of commotion must have been caused by the men opening the roof?

3. Whose faith does Jesus commend? What do we know of the paralytic's faith? Does this surprise you?

◆ **4.** When Jesus says that the man's sins are forgiven, what do you think must have been the reaction of the man and his friends?

◆ **5.** What were the religious leaders thinking? How do you suppose Jesus could tell?

♦ **6.** How did the religious leaders react? Why? Was their argument sound?

♦ **7.** What answer do you suppose Jesus expected from his question: "Which is easier: to say, 'Your sins are forgiven,' or to say, 'Get up and walk'?" Why did Jesus ask this question anyway?

8. What was the man's reaction? What was the crowd's reaction? How would you have responded?

♦ **9.** How do you know Jesus was hard for the people of his day to deal with? What makes him hard for you to deal with? What are some things that might help you?

JESUS LOVES SINNERS

Luke 7:36-50

The best class of people hangs out with only the best class of people. Right? After all, as the Earl of Chesterfield once said, you tend to "take the tone of the company that you are in."

But Jesus surprised normal society. He had a way of setting the tone of those around him. And he somehow changed those considered outcasts into the best of company. On the other hand, he called respected religious leaders proud hypocrites! And just as he challenged them, he challenges us: to which class of people do we belong?

♦ 1. Imagine that you are invited to a dinner party. Not only are your kind of people there, so are some folks from "across the tracks." Some of them seem to have crashed the party. How do you feel?

Read Luke 7:36-50.

♦ **2.** Describe the situation of verses 36-38. What is odd about it?

♦ **3.** How does Jesus explain the woman's actions? Do you think this is the first time she has met Jesus? Why?

♦ **4.** Jesus again seems to know what someone around him— this time Simon—is thinking. Is there any reason for him to draw this conclusion? Why do you suppose he responded with a story?

♦ **5.** What does Jesus want Simon to conclude about the woman? About Simon himself?

♦ **6.** How does this passage fulfill what Isaiah prophesied about Jesus (Luke 4:18-19)?

♦ **7.** What light does this passage shed on Mark's summary of Jesus' message: "The time has come. . . . The kingdom of God is near. Repent and believe the good news" (Mark 1:15)?

♦ **8.** What does this passage imply about sinners? Who can have their sins forgiven? What is required of sinners before this can happen?

9. Jesus said that we who have been forgiven much will love much. Think about an action or attitude for which you really want and need forgiveness. If you were to ask Jesus to forgive you for it, what would you want to do to show him your love and gratitude when he did forgive you?

♦ **10.** If you can, ask Jesus to forgive you for the thing you have been thinking about. Now imagine him saying, "Your sins are forgiven," just as he said to the woman at Simon's house. Can you believe he really forgives you?

WHAT IS SIN ANYWAY?

Mark 7:1-23

Sir Alan Patrick Herbert once wrote:

Don't tell my mother I'm living in sin,
Don't let the old folks know:
Don't tell my twin that I breakfast on gin,
He'd never survive the blow.

A clever rhyme, isn't it? But it brings up a serious question. What is sin, after all? Is it just doing something bad, like stealing or committing adultery? In this passage we'll explore what Jesus thought about the religious leaders' definition of sin.

♦ **1.** Is the subject of sin taken seriously in ordinary conversation among the people you live and work with? When a sin is mentioned, what are some of the things people say or do in reaction?

Read Mark 7:1-23.

2. Who are the various characters and groups mentioned in this passage? What sparks the discussion, and what is the issue?

♦ **3.** Why do you suppose Jesus' reply to the religious leaders was so harsh?

♦ **4.** What does the quotation from Isaiah 29:13 add to Jesus' own words?

♦ **5.** What illustrations does Jesus give of their hypocrisy? Can you explain Corban? How do we today sometimes emphasize appearance over reality?

6. According to Jesus, what makes a person unclean? Where does uncleanliness come from? What does this say about human nature?

◆ **7.** What specific "sins" does Jesus list (verses 21-22)? Which are actions? Which are attitudes? Which seem major to you? Which minor? Does Jesus make any such distinctions? Can you suggest why?

8. Which sins, if any, are you surprised to find there? Why do you suppose Jesus listed them?

◆ **9.** Can you look at this list and honestly say that you have not sinned?

◆ **10.** This passage itself seems not to contain any "good news." How is this bad news countered by what we have learned of Jesus in Luke 7:36-50 and Mark 1:14-15?

◆ **11.** Think about your own everyday habits and encounters. What would you need to change in order to put things into the perspective Jesus had? How do you think you could start to make those changes?

THE GOOD TEACHER

Luke 10:25-37

"It came to me while I was singing . . . that the way to men's souls was through their hearts, not through their minds. As much as a man might be convinced in his mind, as long as his heart remained unchanged all persuasion would fail.

Perhaps it is how we are made; perhaps words of truth reach us best through the heart, and stories and songs are the language of the heart."
—**Steve Lawhead**

No one in Jesus' day told stories like he did. It is one of the characteristics that even otherwise skeptical scholars are willing to attribute to him alone. Here we will look at one of his most famous parables, focusing not only on the teaching in the parable but on the way in which the story teaches a truth about how God wants us to live.

♦ **1.** Who do you think your neighbor is? Does it include only those in close proximity to you? Everyone in need? Only people like you? Or people everywhere?

Read Luke 10:25-37.

2. How important is the subject of the lawyer's first question? With what attitude did the lawyer ask it?

3. Why do you suppose Jesus answered a question with a question?

♦ **4.** What does the lawyer's answer and Jesus' response show about the lawyer's understanding? (See Deuteronomy 6:5 and Leviticus 19:18.)

5. What then was lacking in the lawyer's life?

♦ **6.** In the parable of the Good Samaritan what kind of people failed to help the man? What is implied by Jesus' choice of this pair of people?

7. To what extent did the Samaritan prove himself a neighbor to the man?

♦ **8.** Why would it be so shocking in Israel for the hero of the story to be a Samaritan? What point is Jesus making?

♦ **9.** Does the story Jesus tells answer the exact question the lawyer asked in verse 29? What question does it answer? Who frames that question?

◆ **10.** Put yourself in the lawyer's place: What has Jesus just done to you? How do you feel?

◆ **11.** Jesus' parables often totally upset the expectations of those who hear them. They are more than clever illustrations. They put their hands in your pockets and take all your money. Reflect on how you feel after trying to answer the question posed at the beginning of the study.

12. What changes will you be making in how you think about neighborliness from now on?

◆ **13.** What do you now think of this man from Nazareth?

THE KINGDOM OF GOD

Luke 6:17-36

What is "the world"? Does it mean the same as "the earth"? It seems like "the world" should count as something more than the mountains and sand and water that make it up.

Jesus came preaching that the "kingdom of God" is near. But just what is meant by the term? What is this kingdom's shape and form? It's all so confusing when we try to think what *really* counts in our lives, our world. In this study of the ethics of the kingdom we will only begin to scratch the surface, but it is important to do at least that. Here Jesus explains a few kingdom norms that should guide the actions of his disciples then and now and bring them closer to seeing the world clearly.

1. Suppose you have just been robbed at gunpoint. How do you feel? What does your sense of justice say? How do you react?

Read Luke 6:17-36.

◆ **2.** What is the setting for Jesus' teaching in this passage? Who is he speaking to primarily (verse 20)?

◆ **3.** The three "blesseds" (verses 20-22) contrast and reinforce the three "woes" (verses 24-26). What is the point of each pair?

◆ **4.** How can it be that the poor have the kingdom of God? Or that the hungry will be satisfied, the mournful happy, those persecuted for the sake of the Son of Man (Jesus) joyful?

◆ **5.** What is required if we are to take Jesus at his word in these beatitudes and woes?

♦ **6.** How are we to treat our enemies (verses 27-28)? Why would Jesus give such commands? Aren't they impossible to carry out?

♦ **7.** Does Jesus' instruction in verses 29-30 seem to make sense? What seems wrong about it? Why?

♦ **8.** How do verses 32-36 provide a reason for the instruction of verses 27-30? (Pay special attention to verse 36.)

9. How is the Golden Rule (verse 31) related to Jesus' instruction in verses 27-30?

10. Before the time of Jesus, Rabbi Hillel said, "What is hateful to you, don't do to others. That is the whole law. The rest is commentary." Jesus put the rule in positive form. What is the difference?

♦ **11.** What characteristic of God the Father is emphasized in the Golden Rule? How is it reflected in the life of Jesus? How is it reflected in your life?

♦ **12.** Will you take Jesus' instructions as your guide? Or better, will you take Jesus as your instructor? Will you let him teach you how to live by these kingdom rules?

FATHER AND SON

Luke 15:1-32

Have you ever caught yourself avoiding someone you've offended because you're afraid *he* will avoid *you* first? We in our defensiveness often do things like that with God. Although we're desperately hoping he will love us, we're afraid our sin will make him despise us, so we despise and reject him first! But is he a vengeful God who pours out wrath on all who cross him? Or, on the other hand, is he a cuddly Teddy bear who always gives out warm fuzzies?

Jesus, who claimed to be so close to God that he could call him "Daddy" *(Abba* in his native tongue of Aramaic), tells a story that shows clearly one very important side of God's character. In Luke this parable is one of three Jesus told in response to the stringent religious leaders of his day who complained that Jesus "welcomes sinners and eats with them" (Luke 15:2). That setting becomes important as we look at just what Jesus' most famous parable means.

♦ **1.** What would be the response of your friends (or parents!) if they discovered that you were seen eating with alleged members of the Mafia on a fairly regular basis and you were not even trying to conceal it?

Read Luke 15:1-32.

♦ **2.** There are three distinct stories here. What is the basic point of the first two? How are the "lost" found? How does that explain Jesus' decision to eat with social outcasts?

♦ **3.** In the story of the Prodigal Son, describe the son's actions. How low did he sink?

4. Why did he decide to return home? What did he plan on saying to his father? What is the most he expected his father to do for him?

5. Describe the father's action. How does he answer his son's request? What does that indicate about the father's character?

6. Why does the father immediately call for a feast? How does this feast parallel the events in the first two stories? What point is being made by all three stories?

◆ **7.** Describe the response of the older son. What does the father do? Why do you think Jesus ended the story of the older son before the son makes his final decision to stay in the field or go in to the feast?

◆ **8.** Recall that this parable was told to the Pharisees who complained about who Jesus associated with. Where might they have seen themselves in the story? How might they be expected to respond?

◆ **9.** Define the concept of repentance using only this passage as an illustration. What role in the concept is played by each of the three principal characters? What must God be like for repentance to work?

◆ **10.** In our day who is lost? Who see themselves as lost? Why is it so difficult to recognize our lostness? Why is recognition of our lostness in itself insufficient to bring us back to God?

◆ **11.** Which son in the parable are you most like? What will you do about it?

JESUS, SERVANT AND SAVIOR

Mark 10:32-45

As Jesus' ministry progresses, the fullness of his mission becomes clearer, at least to us who have the benefit of knowing how it all turned out. Prior to Jesus' resurrection, however, things weren't so clear. In the present study we again see Jesus upsetting expectations and giving his disciples more than a glimpse of the deep purpose of his life and death.

◆ **1.** Imagine yourself as one of Jesus' followers. You have been with him for a couple of years in Galilee and have seen how he has angered the religious authorities, especially those from headquarters in Jerusalem. How would you feel about going to Jerusalem at Passover time?

Read Mark 10:32-45.

♦ **2.** Explain the reason for the reaction of the disciples and others who were on their way to Jerusalem.

♦ **3.** To whom did Jesus give the special teaching about his future? Why do you suppose he "took them aside"?

♦ **4.** After hearing Jesus' words in verses 33-34, how appropriate is the request made by James and John?

◆ **5.** Why does Jesus answer them with the question, "Can you drink the cup I drink or be baptized with the baptism I am baptized with?" What should have been their answer?

◆ **6.** What do Jesus' words really predict about the future of James and John? Do you think they understand this prediction?

◆ **7.** What teaching does Jesus give in light of the incident? What significance does it have for people today who believe in Jesus? For those who are still considering whether to follow Christ?

8. How is this "teaching" worked out in Jesus' own life?

♦ **9.** Jesus' comment that he came "to give his life a ransom for many" is one of his most explicit explanations of the reason for his life and death. What does this phrase mean?

♦ **10.** Jesus clearly seems to have had in mind the Servant Song of Isaiah 52:13–53:12, especially Isaiah 53:5 and 10. Read this passage. What sort of person other than one telling the truth would associate himself with the suffering servant of Isaiah?

♦ **11.** Put yourself in the place of James and John, who understood at least partially what Jesus was saying in Mark 10:45. What would you ask for?

WHO IS IN CHARGE HERE?

Mark 11:27–12:12

"It is not wrong to ask questions," some say, "but it is wrong to keep asking them when you already know the answer." Have you noticed how the religious authorities of Jesus' time disregarded this important guideline? Jesus goes to Jerusalem knowing that the religious authorities there are hostile to him and his teaching. This study begins with their challenge to his authority. They ask the same question they've been asking all along—what right does he have to do all these upsetting things?

Jesus' ensuing encounter with these religious leaders provides the context for another of his famous parables. At the same time it reminds us who Jesus is: the one with authority.

♦ **1.** When someone makes an outlandish statement or claim—like saying they know how to solve the problem of the national debt or how to prevent all future wars or how to cure AIDS—what is your first response?

Read Mark 11:27-33.

2. What is the setting for the challenge to Jesus' authority? Who challenged Jesus? Why would they do this?
(See verses 1-18 for events which were public knowl-
edge; verses 19-25 record an event and teaching which
was limited to his disciples.)

3. Why do you think Jesus answered their question with a
question?

♦ **4.** Why is the response of the authorities to John the Baptist relevant?

◆ **5.** How does the answer given by the "authorities" reveal their real concerns? What is revealed about their personal character?

Read Mark 12:1-12.

◆ **6.** This parable is told to those who had questioned Jesus. In light of what you have seen in Mark 11:27-33, why do you think they "knew he had spoken the parable against them" (verse 12)?

◆ **7.** First consider strictly the story Jesus tells—not its application to the situation facing Jesus. What is its main point?

8. How did Jesus apply this main point to the situation he faced as he was telling the story (Mark 10:11)?

9. Who do you think Jesus intended to be identified as "the stone the builders rejected"?

◆ **10.** What other links do you see between the story and Jesus' situation? Who, for instance, does the owner of the vineyard represent? The vineyard itself? (See Isaiah 5:1-7.) The tenants? The owner's servants? The owner's son? The others?

♦ **11.** What links do you see between this parable and our situation today?

♦ **12.** To whom does God choose to give his kingdom?

♦ **13.** For reflection: The authorities "left him and went away." What will you do with Jesus?

THE CRUCIFIXION

Mark 14–15

The story of the arrest, trial, and crucifixion of Jesus is told in all four Gospels. Mark's account was probably the first to be written. Some readers have speculated that Mark himself is the young man who fled naked when Jesus was arrested (Mark 14:51-52). This study surveys the events and points out their significance to our grasp of who Jesus is and what he has accomplished by his death.

♦ **1.** When you think of Jesus' trial and crucifixion, what stands out in your mind? Why?

Read Mark 14.

♦ **2.** In Mark 14:1-31, what reactions do the following people have to Jesus? Why? What was Jesus' reaction to each of them?

The chief priests and teachers (verses 1-2, 10-11)

Judas (verses 10-11)

The woman with the jar of perfume (verses 3-9)

The disciples at the Last Supper (verses 12-31)

Peter (verses 27-31; see also 15:66-72)

3. Among the people and groups listed in question 3, with which do you find yourself in most sympathy? Why?

♦ **4.** What does Jesus know about what is going to happen to him and what it will mean? Look especially at verses 6-9, 22-25, 35-36.

♦ **5.** Describe the testimony given in Jesus' trial before the Sanhedrin (the chief ruling body of the Jews). What is the main charge against him? How does he reply to it?

Read Mark 15.

♦ **6.** What is the charge before Pilate (the head of the Roman government in Jerusalem)? How does he reply? What is Pilate's dilemma? How does he try to resolve it?

7. In what sense is Jesus "king of the Jews"?

♦ **8.** What happens while Jesus is on the cross? What does he say? Why? (Recall Jesus' teaching about servanthood [Mark 10:45], his comment at the Last Supper [Mark 14:24], and his prayer in the Garden of Gethsemane [Mark 14:36].)

9. Verses 42-47 describe Jesus' burial. Why do you think it is important to know that Jesus was really dead?

♦ **10.** How did Jesus impress the centurion? Why do you suppose Mark included his comment? How does the centurion's comment challenge us today?

THE
RESURRECTION

Luke 24

Your neighbor has just told you that last night he saw a flying saucer land in his back yard. Some strange aliens took him aboard and gave him a whirlwind tour of the entire earth. Imagine your reaction. It may not be so different from that of the first time Jesus' contemporaries heard about his resurrection.

When the apostle Paul mentioned the resurrection of Jesus to the philosophers in Athens, some of them "sneered." And well they might! Some still do. After all, such a thing just couldn't happen. Or could it? The united testimony of the first disciples, the apostle Paul, and the four Gospels is that indeed it did happen. Paul even argues (1 Corinthians 15) that the whole of the Christian faith hinges on its happening. Our picture of Jesus would not be complete without seeing his death lead to his resurrection. In this study we will look at some of the evidence.

1. Imagine you are returning to the grave of a person you have seen buried a few days earlier. When you get there you find an open pit and an open casket with no body in it. How would you react?

Read Luke 24.

◆ **2.** Who first discovers that the tomb is empty? Given the first-century opinion that the testimony of women was not worth much, why do you think Luke mentions them?

◆ **3.** How likely is it that the women went to the wrong tomb? (See Luke 23:55-56.)

4. Where does the first explanation of the empty tomb come from? Why does the explanation make sense to the women?

◆ **5.** What is the reaction of the disciples? Of Peter in particular?

◆ **6.** What additional detail does the Gospel of John 20:3-9 add to Luke 24:12? What is the significance of the way the grave clothes were lying?

7. What happened on the road to Emmaus? What did the two disciples reveal about their former hopes? Why do you suppose Jesus taught them out of the Scriptures (the Old Testament)? Why did he do so before they recognized him? How did their experience affect them?

♦ **8.** How does Jesus finally resolve the confusion of the disciples? What is the value of the evidence given in verses 37-43?

♦ **9.** What is Jesus primarily interested in teaching the disciples after his resurrection? What is their role to be?

10. One test of a person's character is the consistency of his life. How consistent is the Resurrection with the claims we have seen Jesus making in earlier studies?

◆ **11.** To summarize, name the kinds of evidence that are given for the Resurrection.

◆ **12.** What do you think of the conclusion of Sir Edward Clarke who wrote as follows to the Rev. E. L. Macassey? "As a lawyer I have made a prolonged study of the evidences for the events of the first Easter Day. To me the evidence is conclusive, and over and over again in the High Court I have secured the verdict on evidence not nearly so compelling. Inference follows on evidence, and a truthful witness is always artless and disdains effect. The Gospel evidence for the resurrection is of this class, and as a lawyer I accept it unreservedly as the testimony of truthful men to facts they were able to substantiate."

♦ **13.** How would you defend the reasonability of the conviction that Jesus rose from the dead?

JESUS THE MESSAGE

Luke 24:45-53; Acts 2:1-41

People who have been through a harsh winter are delighted and relieved when spring comes. People who have been through a severe illness treasure being able to run, to eat, to breathe fresh air. And those who have lost their sight comment how they hardly noticed colors and shapes until they were unable to see them. Think about it—sometimes, it seems, we have to know the darkness before we can appreciate the light.

We've seen how Jesus knew the darkness—he experienced one of the most horrible, torturous deaths imaginable. And his disciples, too, knew great sorrow and fear as they were left for a short while without their friend and leader. But then Jesus conquered death, and their excitement and joy, as we will see in this study, was impossible to contain. How could they help but share his message of light with the world?

1. What are some ways in which you have experienced a "resurrection"? How did you relate this experience to others?

Read Luke 24:45-53.

♦ **2.** How does Luke leave the disciples at the end of his Gospel? If you had been one of Jesus' followers at that point, how would you feel about the future?

Read Acts 2:1-41.

♦ **3.** The author of Luke is also the author of Acts. With what events does Luke begin his narrative (Acts 1)?

♦ **4.** How are the events of verses 1-13 the fulfillment of Luke 24:49 and Acts 1:4-5, 8?

♦ **5.** In addition to the followers of Jesus, who else is there (verses 5-13)? What is their reaction to what is happening?

6. What is the immediate context in which Peter begins his sermon? How does he explain the phenomena?

♦ **7.** How interested is Peter in the phenomena as such? What topic is Peter more interested in explaining?

♦ **8.** How does Peter summarize Jesus' life? How does he indicate that his listeners have already been involved with Jesus?

♦ **9.** On what aspect of Jesus' life does Peter concentrate? How does he explain it? Why would this explanation have some credibility among his listeners?

10. How do Peter's remarks in verse 36 both summarize his message and call for a response from his audience? What response does Peter believe is appropriate?

♦ **11.** What similarities and differences are there between Peter's challenge in verse 39 and Jesus' message in Mark 1:15?

♦ **12.** What does Peter say will happen to those who accept the challenge of verse 38?

13. How universal does Peter consider his challenge and the promise of verse 38 to be (see verse 39)?

♦ **14.** Think back over all the things you've learned in this studyguide. What do you think of Jesus? What implications does his life have for you?

LEADER'S NOTES

■ Study 1/ Enter Jesus

The purpose of this study is to introduce you or your group to Jesus.
Mark's gospel has been chosen because it gets the reader into the
life and teaching of Jesus very quickly. Scholars generally agree that
it was written around A.D. 64-65. For readers who are skeptical of
the historical reliability of the Gospels, I recommend Paul Barnett,
Is the New Testament History? (Downers Grove: InterVarsity Press,
1986); F. F. Bruce, *The New Testament Documents: Are They Reli-
able?* 6th ed. (Downers Grove: InterVarsity Press, 1981); and Craig
L. Blomberg, *The Historical Reliability of the Gospels* (Downers
Grove: InterVarsity Press, 1987). The most helpful commentary on
Mark is William L. Lane, *The Gospel of Mark* (Grand Rapids:
Eerdmans, 1974).

You will find more comments in this study than in future ones for
two reasons: (1) If you are leading a group for the first time, they
will help you to get a feel for the kinds of answers expected from
the questions; and (2) some of the concepts in this study—especially
the notion of the kingdom of God—are more complex and unusual
than concepts in later studies.

Question 1. This question sets the stage for seeing Mark's opening as intriguing, for the likelihood is that most people will think that the "beginning of the gospel about Jesus" (Mark 1:1) will be his birth. For Mark, it isn't.

Question 2. Mark sets Jesus quickly but firmly in the prophetic tradition of Judaism. Not only is Jesus predicted, but his forerunning prophet has been predicted as well.

Question 3. Note specific ways in which John fulfills what Isaiah prophesied. He was a *messenger ahead* (Mark 1:2) of Jesus—his message was, *"After me* will come one . . ." (verse 7) He *prepared the way* (verses 2-3) for Jesus' ministry—he came "preaching a baptism of repentance for the forgiveness of sins," and the people confessed their sins (verses 4-5). He lived in the desert (verses 3-4)—he even dressed roughly like a man of the desert (verse 6). Perhaps you can present this question: What does this prophet-messenger mean when he says, "Prepare the way for the Lord"?

Question 4. The Holy Spirit breaks through from heaven, and the voice identifies Jesus as his "Son." Then the Spirit sends Jesus into the desert.

Question 5. An episode in a cosmic battle with evil takes place as Jesus wrestles with Satan and is ministered to by angels. See Matthew 4:1-17 if you'd like to know more about this time of temptation in Jesus' life.

Question 6. Mark 1:16-20. Notice how Jesus simply says, "Come, follow me," and the disciples do it. Isn't this a picture of what good subjects in a kingdom do when addressed by the king? Here we see how Jesus has authority over *people.*

Verses 21-28. In this section Jesus encounters an evil spirit, and the spirit seems to be very much afraid of him. With a stern command, Jesus calls it out of the man it is torturing, and the people are so amazed at his power and his teaching that they spread the news about him all over the region. We can see how Jesus has authority over the *spirit realm*.

Verses 29-32. Jesus is compassionate to his friend's mother-in-law, and, because of his power in healing her, the people of the town come to his door wanting him to heal their sick. Note how gently he works—he takes the elderly lady's hand, helps her up, and she is healed. It's not the picture we usually look for when we encounter power, and yet the results are obvious: Jesus has authority over *disease*.

Question 7. Mark obviously has a high view of Jesus, identifying him immediately as the "Son of God" (Mark 1:1). Note that the evidence supplied by each section supports this designation, as do the views of the "voice from heaven" and the evil spirit.

Question 9. As leader of the group, challenge each participant in your study to grapple with the message of the Gospels as they go through this series of studies till they have settled in their own minds whether Mark and the other Gospel writers are right.

■ Study 2/Jesus Visits Nazareth

Luke 4:14-30 sets the opening of Jesus' ministry in his own hometown. It shows not only that Jesus had an explicit agenda for his ministry, but that he associated himself with three of the great prophets of old. In fact, Jesus claimed that what Isaiah saw as his own mission was not really fulfilled until he himself arrived on the scene.

The purpose of this study is to show how Jesus exasperated the people of his hometown, and through this to show how he upsets our expectations as well. In this passage Jesus leaves us no third choice: he is either who he says he is—the fulfiller of Israel's hopes—or he is a very deluded or very evil man. One value of using Luke to present Jesus' case for himself is that Luke is acknowledged to be an accurate historian. For those skeptical of this, I suggest reading "Luke the Historian," chapter 7 of F. F. Bruce's *The New Testament Documents: Are They Reliable?* (See Selected Bibliography at the end of this studyguide.) More detail is found in I. H. Marshall, *Luke the Historian* (Grand Rapids: Eerdmans, 1970). The most helpful commentary on Luke is I. H. Marshall, *Commentary on Luke* (Grand Rapids: Eerdmans, 1978).

Question 1. This question sets the stage for bridging the gap between Jesus' time and our own. People in the Bible are quite similar to us in their psychological make-up. The more we can see this, the more obvious it becomes that the Bible is telling us the truth about ourselves even when we don't like it.

Question 2. Get a quick, obvious answer to this question and move on to the next, where the implications are addressed.

Question 3. Encourage someone in the group to imagine one of their friends returning from college and making a claim to be the one who would, after all these years of cultural decline, be the one to reform the world.

Question 4. His listeners assumed that they were God's chosen, while actually they were outside the kingdom of God and didn't realize it. Only by realizing their own poverty could Jesus' listeners participate in the kingdom of God.

Question 6. Here Jesus associates his own action and the action of the great prophets of old with help for people of other nations. The current attitude of Israelis to Lebanese and Syrians helps illustrate this passage.

Question 7. Note how Jesus' way of controlling the situation is consistent with his teaching (see Matthew 5–6.) He doesn't try to hurt his enemies. Rather, he quietly leaves them.

Question 8. His neighbors could only believe him or think him crazy or blasphemous.

Question 9. Jesus wanted to make it clear that he was making extreme claims for himself—his identity, his authority. He wanted a full acceptance of himself without reservations—a rather unnatural thing to expect, as the proverb he quotes suggests.

Question 10. Our choices are indeed the same as they were for Jesus' neighbors. Either we can reject him and his teaching entirely, or we can accept him and follow what he says. The biggest step toward acceptance is believing that Jesus is who he said he was; then, it's much easier to believe what he taught. Ask your group this question: Is this something you think you can accept?

■ Study 3/Jesus Forgives Sins

This passage has been selected to focus on Jesus' claim to forgive sins. It is a key element in Jesus' self-understanding, for if he thought he could forgive sins, he was taking onto himself an ability God alone could have. Thus he was implicitly claiming either to be divine or to be acting on behalf of God. No good Jew—rabbi or ordinary person—would do that.

Question 1. These questions will help group members apply the study later, as well as lead them to see how Jesus is God, whom we offend when we sin. If participants have trouble coming to the conclusion that only the offended party can forgive the offender, have them think of a person they've offended. Then say, "Hey, it's okay. I forgive you for that." Do they feel forgiven? Of course not! Discuss, too, how even if the offender apologizes or agrees to pay for the damage, a person is not obliged to forgive him or her. The act of forgiveness comes from the heart of the offended person.

Question 2. The idea here is to set in the mind of the participants the drama of the event.

Question 4. This is a speculative question, but the presumption is that they all wanted a physical cure and would have been surprised at Jesus' remark.

Question 5. The Pharisees were a religious sect of Jews bent on a strict interpretation of the Law, and most teachers of the law were Pharisees. It stands to reason that they would be upset, and since Jesus knew the Law very well (and could probably see angry looks on their faces), we can be sure he knew exactly what they would think even before the words came out of his mouth.

Question 6. Actually, the reaction of the religious leaders is well founded. Only the one offended can forgive the offending one. When Jesus says that the man's sins (offenses against God) are forgiven, he is making an implicit claim to divinity. Only God could make such a declaration.

Question 7. Actually, anyone could *say* either one. It is the *doing* of either that is the difficult task. One can of course be observed; the other cannot. And this is in fact why he asks the question. If he can heal the paralytic—that is, act as physical healer—there is reason to believe that he can also act as spiritual healer.

Question 9. Use these questions to spark a summary of your group's discovery so far.

■ Study 4/Jesus Loves Sinners

This study focuses on Jesus' compassion for sinners. There is no sinner so sinful that repentance is not possible. And with repentance comes love for him who forgives.

Question 1. Spend some time discussing the social awkwardness of finding people at dinner parties you don't think deserve to be there.

Question 2. The woman comes to anoint Jesus with perfume but seems to have been overcome with emotion and instead begins weeping, her tears falling on Jesus' feet. (Jesus would have been reclining to dine, as was the custom at formal dinners.)

Question 3. Jesus says the woman loves him because he has forgiven her sins. Apparently the woman has met Jesus before and he has already forgiven her sins. She has now sought him out to express her appreciation. At the end of the dialogue, then, Jesus reassures her of that forgiveness (Luke 7:48).

Question 4. Jesus often taught in parables—clever stories designed to uncover a truth, often a truth about the person to whom Jesus was speaking. Try discussing how we are often more willing to believe what someone is teaching us if we are involved in the discovery process. Here Jesus involves Simon in the judgment about the quality of love forgiven sinners can be expected to display.

Question 5. He wants Simon to see that the woman has been forgiven and that Simon has not. Only the ones who recognize their own sin can be forgiven. Simon does not recognize his own sin. This is a condition worse than that of the woman whose sins are so obvious to Simon and society at large.

Question 6. The woman is not monetarily poor (she has a flask of expensive perfume), but she has been a prisoner of her profession, and Jesus has set her free.

Question 7. The events of this passage illustrate how the kingdom of God comes near when forgiveness is granted. The "news" for the woman is very "good" indeed.

Question 8. Anyone can have his or her sins forgiven. Repentance—sorrow for sin and turning away from its practice—is the only requirement.

Question 10. This is a thought question. Do not require participants to answer unless they wish. Some who are just learning about Jesus may be overcome with emotion as they reflect on this passage. Some may be so troubled by guilt for past sins that this passage leads them to repentance and acceptance of Jesus as their Savior. Be prepared to help anyone who would like to do that.

This encounter with Jesus can be made concrete by praying the following prayer:

> Heavenly Father, I know that I am a sinner and have offended you by what I have said and done. I am grieved by that. I do not

deserve your love or your forgiveness. But I know that in Jesus Christ you forgive sinners. So I believe in him and put my trust in him. I want to live from now on under your care and in obedience to you. Please accept me as one of your children and live in me by your Holy Spirit. Help me live as you want me to. In the name of Jesus Christ, Amen.

Be sensitive to each person in the group. *Do not require anyone to pray such a prayer.* There is nothing automatic about repentance or salvation. The impulse to repent must come from the heart of each person (even if that impulse is put there by the Holy Spirit).

■ Study 5/What Is Sin Anyway?

This study examines the nature of sin. Sin, we learn, is an attitude as much as an action; it originates from our own hearts; all of us are caught up in it. So all of us stand condemned by God. We must therefore rely on God's grace in Jesus Christ to forgive us and set us free from sin's bondage and habits.

Question 1. Be careful not to let your group get into a discussion about *which* things are actually *sins.* The point here is to notice how people react to sin in general: do they ignore it? Do they laugh about it? Are they uncomfortable, or do they speak out against it?

Question 3. Jesus is always harder on the self-righteous than on the sinners who know they are sinners (recall Simon in Luke 7:36-50).

Question 4. It grounds Jesus' teaching in the very tradition they thought they were upholding and shows Jesus' respect for that tradition.

Question 5. The term *Corban* means money devoted to God by an oath. Though respect for parents was at the heart of the law, a selfish son could promise the temple the money that would normally have been given for the care of parents, and so avoid his duty. It will be helpful for group members to discuss how we also are guilty of hypocrisy today.

Question 7. It is helpful to see the panorama of sins listed; there are many kinds—so-called major, so-called minor, internal and external. Jesus makes no distinction between them because all sin is sin.

Question 9. The apostle Paul put the same point this way: "For all have sinned and fall short of the glory of God" (Romans 3:23).

Question 10. It may help for someone in the group to summarize what has been learned earlier in studies 1, 3, and 4.

Question 11. As at the end of the previous study, some participants may be ready to repent. You may wish to refer to the Leader's Notes in study 4, question 10.

■ **Study 6/The Good Teacher**

This study takes a risk. The first question asks participants the same question that the lawyer asked Jesus. It got him in deep trouble. He discovered it was the wrong question to ask. So as you begin this study, treat the members in your group with some compassion, for your questions will lead them astray. All their calculations of just how far afield one might go to find a neighbor is couched in the rhetoric of the kingdom of darkness. When this dawns on them, they may be angry with you or with this guide. So proceed with caution!

Question 1. Let participants air their views and argue a bit with each other if they disagree, then gently ask them to take a look at what happened when a lawyer asked Jesus the same question.

Question 4. Jesus himself summed up the commandments in similar terms in Mark 12:28-34. So the lawyer understood the essence of the law.

Question 6. The priest and Levite (a member of a lesser order of temple officials) represent those in society who are thought to be and generally claim to be righteous. Jesus was showing how those who are "supposed" to do right often don't.

Question 8. In the history of Israel, the Jews were captured and taken as prisoners of war, in a sense, away from their land. As a final blow to this elitist nation, their captors sent foreigners to live where they once had. These strangers intermarried with many of the Jews who had been left behind, and they settled in Samaria. The Israelites despised these Samaritans, much in the way the Israelis disdain the Palestinians today, because they were not pureblood Jews and had taken over their land. So Jesus was causing quite a stir here!

Question 9. Jesus frames the question that his story answers. Help participants to see that Jesus shows that the lawyer's question is the wrong one. To answer it would take moral calculus. God's righteousness is not to be determined that way. The real issue is whether the lawyer will be a neighbor.

Questions 10-11. These questions are designed to get the group to reflect on how the parable strikes them and to consider again their view of Jesus. Meeting Jesus the parable-teller can be a frightening thing.

Question 13. The final question raises again the issue of each study: What will you do with Jesus?

■ Study 7/The Kingdom of God

The primary purpose of this study is to help people see the seemingly outlandish instructions Jesus often gives to his disciples. They go against the grain of normal ethical teaching and require action that at first just seems crazy. Thus they again raise the question: Who is this man? He is either insane, deluding us deliberately, or somehow wise beyond our understanding. Yet, as we reflect on his teaching in the present passage, the wisdom of his teaching begins to break through our consciousness.

Question 2. "Disciples" can be thought of in a few different ways. We call the twelve men he singled out, who spent all their time with him for the three years of his ministry, his disciples. There was also a group of seventy followers that adhered to his teaching and regularly spent time with him (this group included many women who took care of Jesus and his friends). Some of these were probably people he had healed and/or forgiven—they may have become disciples out of gratitude as much as conviction that Jesus was the Messiah the Jews had been waiting for. A final group of disciples were the people who had encountered Jesus once or a few times and believed him wholeheartedly. Whenever he was near their town, they went along with the curiosity-seekers to greet him and listen to his teachings. Luke 6:20 could be talking about any of these groups.

Questions 3-4. The answer to question 3 is obvious. The answer to question 4 is not. Your group may be puzzled. Some may try to spiritualize the "poor" by noting that in the Sermon on the Mount Jesus himself says "poor in spirit" (Matthew 5:3). It is best to leave the puzzle unsolved. Somehow Jesus is telling us that our values—wealth, food, laughter, ease in life—are not primary. Something else is more important—to see ourselves in really desperate need. To be satisfied now is to be left out in the cold when his kingdom comes in fullness and power.

Question 5. We must trust him to be telling the truth because he is a truthteller who knows beyond our knowing, that is, because on these matters he has the mind of God.

Question 6. Jesus gives us such commands because they reflect the ethics of the kingdom of God. This is the way God's people are to live. The fact that his people are yet unable to obey perfectly does not lower the standard. It should rather cause us to seek God's mercy (verse 36).

Question 7. Jesus' instruction in verses 29-30 violates our sense of justice. The one who rips us off, we feel, should be punished, not get a blessing from us.

Question 8. Verses 32-36 remind us that God is merciful; we should be like him in that quality. Being a "son of the Most High" is our reward.

Question 11. The mercy or grace of God is central. We know as well that he is always just, but the working out of that justice is in his hands, not ours. God says, "It is mine to avenge; I will repay" (Hebrews 10:30).

Question 12. The final question raises again the issue of each study: What will you do with Jesus?

■ Study 8/Father and Son

The parable of the Prodigal Son is deservedly famous. Within its brief compass is displayed a rich insight into the character of God—the longing of God the Father for the lost, his joy at their repentance, his graciousness in forgiving, the lavishness of his response to the repentant. It also shows a profound insight into the human psychology of sin and repentance. Its central message should not be missed: God is waiting to receive his wayward children; they need only recognize their lostness, turn around, and come back to him.

Question 1. It may help to note that the Pharisees had a rule against sharing "table-fellowship with those whom they considered sinful" (Marshall, *Commentary on Luke,* p. 599). Yet Jesus frequently dined with sinners (see Luke 5:30-31, where he explains why).

Question 2. Do not spend much time with this question. The main point of the study is in the third story.

Question 3. To the Jews pigs are unclean animals, not to be raised or eaten.

Questions 7-8. The Pharisees would almost surely see themselves as the older son. They had not left home. They were the guardians of the household. Perhaps Jesus left the older son in the field—undecided—to indicate that a choice could always be made to celebrate the graciousness and mercy of the father.

Question 9. Emphasize here the need for God's grace.

Questions 10-11. Help participants deal with their own stance before God. If some need help in turning from their old ways, you may find the Leader's Notes for question 10 in study 4 helpful.

■ Study 9/Jesus, Servant and Savior

Question 1. Your group should have picked up by now that Jesus was constantly under pressure from the religious authorities and that it would be dangerous to go to their headquarters.

Question 2. The disciples might be expected to have considerable confidence in Jesus and yet wonder what even more striking things might happen to Jesus and to them in Jerusalem.

Question 3. Mark emphasizes Jesus' reluctance to make his ultimate role as Messiah an open teaching. But he wants to prepare his specially chosen disciples for what is about to occur.

Question 4. The two disciples do not grasp what Jesus has said. They believe that Jesus is going to be a political Messiah and restore the political throne of David; they want a place of honor in that reign.

Question 5. The question of Mark 10:38 calls for a negative reply. The "cup" and the "baptism" refer to Jesus' suffering and death. In study 14 we'll see how everyone deserted Jesus when he was arrested. Obviously, James and John weren't ready to face all that Jesus did.

Question 6. Acts 12:2 tells of the death of James at the hands of Herod. Revelation 1:9 speaks of John's exile and suffering for the sake of Christ.

Question 7. This question raises the cost of commitment; for the believer it is a call to serve; for the one considering faith in Christ it emphasizes the cost.

Question 9. Jesus' death is the sacrifice for our sins. Paul elaborates on the concept in Romans 5:6-9.

Question 10. This question is designed to bring the group back to a point made in earlier studies: someone who thinks of himself in terms of the suffering servant of Isaiah is either liar, lunatic, or Lord.

Question 11. Here the point is to bring home to the participants the implications of Jesus as a ransom for them.

■ Study 10/Who Is in Charge Here?

One issue in this study is Jesus' authority. It is important to note just how much authority Jesus claimed for himself. The more personal issue regards the citizens of the kingdom of God: Will we be among them?

Question 1. The issue is one of authority: Why should we believe them? Who gave them the right to make such claims?

Questions 4-5. These questions are designed to help group members see that Jesus calls people to the consequences of their beliefs. They have, of course, rejected the message of John the Baptist. But John (Luke 3:7-20) preached the same kind of judgment as Jesus executed in the overturning of the money changers' tables (Mark 11:15-17).

Question 6. This question is to be used as a discussion starter—an overall focus for the questions to follow. Do not spend much time on it; the discussion of the remaining questions will make the answer clear.

Question 7. The answers you get here may reflect a variety of emphases; for example, that some tenants don't have the good of their owner in mind, that people are greedy, that fortunes can be dramatically reversed, that justice wins in the end. It is the latter two of these that are most important to see. Someone in your group may comment that the story is unrealistic: How could they think that if they killed the son they would inherit the vineyard? Actually, the story reflects Galilean custom; in Jesus' day there was provision in the law that if a landlord left no heirs, the land could fall to them.

Question 10. There are a number of allegorical elements in Jesus' story. Some of them would certainly be recognized by the people listening: owner—God; vineyard—Israel; tenants—the religious authorities themselves; owner's servants—the prophets of old (including the recent John the Baptist). It is not so clear that they would have understood Jesus as the Son, for the Messiah was not commonly thought to be a "son" of God. Mark, however, clearly sees this and expects his readers to do so. The story also pictures what would happen to Jesus in just a short time—his crucifixion (Mark 12:8) and his resurrection (Mark 12:10-11).

Question 11. Don't let the discussion get bogged down in identifying today's false religious leaders. The point must be more personal. Are we among those who are rejecting Jesus' authority in our lives? How?

Question 12. Someone should point out that God gives his kingdom to those who accept his authority and the authority of his Son.

Question 13. You may wish to use this simply as a question to go unanswered by discussion. Be prepared to help those in your group who would at this point like to make a first commitment to Jesus, to yield for the first time to his authority. See the Leader's Notes to study 4 for help.

■ Study 11/The Crucifixion

The passage studied here is quite long, and your group cannot linger long over any one section. The main point of the study is to show that Jesus alone knew what was going to happen to him and what it would mean—his death and separation from the Father, as the ransom for us. Many other lessons could be drawn from the material and will be by various members of the group, but keep the focus on the main one.

Question 1. It is most important here to get responses from those who are still considering faith in Christ or those who are relatively new believers. Older Christians may want to expand on what they say. Try not to let them. It will get in the way of looking at the details in Mark's Gospel.

Question 2. If you can, divide the group into five subsections and have each investigate one of the people or groups. After a couple of minutes, take up each in turn.

Question 4. This question points to Jesus' awareness of the awesome ordeal he is about to undergo—the suffering for the sins of human-kind. Someone may note the connection between Jesus' prayer in Mark 14:36 and his cry from the cross in 15:34.

Questions 5-6. These questions are designed to bring out the irony in Mark's Gospel. Jesus is who he says he is charged with being— "the Christ, the Son of the Blessed One" (Mark 14:61), "the Son of Man" (14:62), and "the king of the Jews" (15:2). But the religious leaders do not realize it nor understand what these terms really mean as they apply to Jesus. For example, Jesus is really "the Son of the Blessed One," and therefore not guilty of blasphemy. He is king, but not of a political realm, and therefore not really guilty by Roman law.

Question 8. Jesus' cry of abandonment indicated the separation from God he experienced because in his death he was bearing the guilt of all humankind's sin. The words themselves are a quotation of the first line of Psalm 22.

Question 10. Again the study closes on a question designed to bring your group face to face with Jesus.

■ Study 12/The Resurrection

One short study is not sufficient to consider all the information the New Testament gives on the resurrection of Jesus. Nor is there space to consider all the objections that have been offered by skeptics. This study is a start. Those who want to go further or who still have some doubts should be encouraged first to read chapter 4 of John R. W. Stott's *Basic Christianity,* 2nd ed. (Downers Grove: InterVarsity Press, 1971), pp. 46-60. There are a number of good books that go into great detail on the Resurrection. Among the best are George Eldon Ladd, *I Believe in the Resurrection of Jesus* (Grand Rapids: Eerdmans, 1975); Michael Green, *The Day Death Died* (London: InterVarsity Press, 1984); and Gary R. Habermas and Antony G. N. Flew, *Did Jesus Rise from the Dead? The Resurrection Debate* (San Francisco: Harper and Row, 1987, a debate between two philosophers—a Christian and a well-known atheist).

Question 2. It establishes the credibility of the account. If it weren't true, no Gospel writer would have invented it for the purposes of testimony.

Question 3. Not very likely. They had seen where he was buried.

Questions 5-6. Many scholars believe the "other disciple" in John 20:3 is the apostle John, the author of the Gospel of John or at least the eyewitness on whom the account is based. John 20:3-9 has the ring of eyewitness testimony. The grave clothes are lying in a position they would have taken if Jesus' body had been transfigured and passed through them. "The body cloths, under the weight of 100 lbs. of spices (John 19:39), once the support of the body had been removed, would have subsided or collapsed, and would now be lying flat. A gap would have appeared between the body cloths and head napkin, where his face and neck had been. And the napkin itself, because of the complicated criss-cross shape, a crumpled turban, but with no head inside" *(Basic Christianity,* p. 53). Some translations do not include Luke 24:12 except in a footnote, holding that it is not in the most reliable manuscripts of Luke.

Question 8. It is important to note that Jesus is not a "ghost" (Luke 24:37) but the same person as the one crucified. The body is no longer in the tomb; it has been transmuted but is in some ways the same body.

Question 9. He wants them to know who he is and that what he has done is a fulfillment of prophecy. The disciples will be witness to what has occurred, and it is implied, when they are "clothed with power from on high" they will "preach repentance and forgiveness of sins" from Jerusalem to all nations.

Question 11. The evidence we have seen here is of six types: (1) the empty tomb (the body is gone), (2) the position of the grave clothes, (3) the post-resurrection appearance of Jesus to his followers, (4) the fulfillment of his own prophecy prior to his death, and (5) the consistency of the Resurrection with his other claims. A fuller study of all the New Testament evidence would include a major additional item: (6) the change in the disciples from weak men to strong leaders willing to undergo persecution and death for their belief in Jesus and his resurrection. (Tradition says most of them died as martyrs.) The apostle Paul summarizes Jesus' post-resurrection appearances in 1 Corinthians 15:3-7.

Question 12. Clarke's remarks are quoted by Stott, *Basic Christianity*, p. 47. The resurrection of Jesus cannot in a strict sense be "proven." There is, however, good evidence for it and good rebuttals for alternative explanations of the data of the New Testament.

Question 13. If any group members still have questions about the Resurrection, refer them to the books mentioned at the beginning of this study's Leader's Notes.

■ Study 13/Jesus the Message

The goal of this series of studies has been to lead people to repentance for their sin and to faith in Jesus Christ as Lord and Savior. Therefore, especially in this final study, you should keep the attention of the group on the major point of Peter's sermon found in Acts 2:38-39. Avoid getting sidetracked on interesting issues that are tangential to the main one. You will want to emphasize that the message of today's disciples is Jesus Christ himself. It is in him we see the kingdom of God draw near, as he said in Mark 1:15. It is in him we have forgiveness of sins. It is in him we see the pattern of life we should live. Keep the attention of your group on these issues.

Questions 2-3. Rather than asking question 2 of the group, you may wish to summarize the events yourself, just to make a quicker transition from the previous study to this one.

Questions 4-5. There will be a tendency for your group to get so interested in the phenomenon of "speaking in other tongues" that you will not have time to consider the main part of the study, which comes in the next section of Acts. After the situation itself is basically understood by your group, move on to the next section.

Question 7. Peter begins with the situation that has attracted attention and then quickly bridges to the real point of his sermon—Jesus himself.

Question 8. Notice that Peter puts the burden of guilt for Jesus' death on those he is talking to, even though they may not personally have been in the crowd that demanded that he die. Discuss with your group why that could be. What implications might it have for each of us today?

Question 9. The Resurrection was the key issue in the message of the early church. The Old Testament formed the text by which events of the recent past could be understood; his audience (Jews who lived all around the Mediterranean but were in Jerusalem for the Passover) would have accepted its basic authority.

Question 11. The key point of difference is the phrase "in the name of Jesus." The message of the early church is going to be Jesus himself. In him the kingdom of God has been brought near.

Question 12. There may be some confusion among those in your group as to what it means to "receive the gift of the Holy Spirit." Essentially it means that God the Holy Spirit comes to dwell within the believer. Sometimes this initial indwelling is accompanied by special phenomena like "talking in tongues"; sometimes not. For further elaboration on this topic, you may wish to refer your group to John R. W. Stott, *Baptism and Fullness: The Work of the Holy Spirit Today,* 2nd ed. (Downers Grove: InterVarsity Press, 1976) or Charles Hummell, *Fire in the Fireplace* (Downers Grove: InterVarsity Press, 1978). Charles Hummel has an excellent short treatment of the topic in his booklet *Filled with the Spirit* (Downers Grove: InterVarsity Press, 1981).

Question 14. You may wish to challenge those in your group who have yet to make a commitment to Jesus to do so now. See the suggestions in the Leader's Notes to study 4 for further help in doing this.

A SELECTED BIBLIOGRAPHY OF BOOKS ON JESUS

■ **I. THE HISTORICAL FIGURE**

Bruce, F. F. *The Real Jesus*. Downers Grove, Ill.: InterVarsity Press, 1985.

Dodd, C. H. *The Founder of Christianity*. New York: Macmillan, 1970.

Habermas, Gary and Antony Flew. *Did Jesus Rise from the Dead?* San Francisco: Harper and Row, 1987.

Ladd, George Eldon. *I Believe in the Resurrection*. Grand Rapids, Mich.: Eerdmans, 1975.

Stein, Robert H. *The Method and Message of Jesus' Teachings*. Philadelphia: Westminster Press, 1978.

Stott, John R. W. *Basic Christianity*. 2nd ed. Downers Grove, Ill.: InterVarsity Press, 1971.

■ **II. THE EVIDENCE FOR THE HISTORICAL FIGURE**

Barnett, Paul. *Is the New Testament History?* Ann Arbor, Mich.: Servant, 1986.

Blomberg, Craig. *Are the Gospels Reliable History?* Downers Grove, Ill.: InterVarsity Press, 1987.

Bruce, F. F. *The New Testament Documents: Are They Reliable?* 6th ed. Downers Grove: InterVarsity Press, 1981.

Dunn, James D. G. *The Evidence for Jesus.* Philadelphia: Fortress, 1985.

France, R. T. *The Evidence for Jesus.* Downers Grove, Ill.: InterVarsity Press, 1986.

Gruenler, Royce Gordon. *New Approaches to Jesus and the Gospels: A Phenomenological and Exegetical Study of Synoptic Christology.* Grand Rapids, Mich.: Baker, 1982.

Barnett, Paul. *Is the New Testament Reliable?* Downer's Grove, Ill.: InterVarsity Press, 1993.

Marshall, I. Howard. *I Believe in the Historical Jesus.* Grand Rapids, Mich.: Eerdmans, 1977.

McDowell, Josh. *Evidence That Demands a Verdict.* Rev. ed. San Bernardino, Calif.: Here's Life, 1979.

———. *More Evidence That Demands a Verdict.* Rev. ed. San Bernardino, Calif.: Here's Life, 1981.

Wenham, John W. *Christ and the Bible.* 2nd ed. Grand Rapids, Mich.: Baker, 1984.

WHAT SHOULD WE STUDY NEXT?

To help your group answer that question, we've listed the Fisherman Guides by category so you can choose your next study.

TOPICAL STUDIES

Becoming Women of Purpose, Barton

Building Your House on the Lord, Brestin

Discipleship, Reapsome

Doing Justice, Showing Mercy, Wright

Encouraging Others, Johnson

Examining the Claims of Jesus, Brestin

Friendship, Brestin

Sermon on the Mount, Hunt

Great Doctrines of the Bible, Board

Great Passages of the Bible, Plueddemann

Great People of the Bible, Plueddemann

Great Prayers of the Bible, Plueddemann

Guidance & God's Will, Stark

Higher Ground, Brestin

How Should a Christian Live? (1, 2, & 3 John), Brestin

Let's Pray Together, Fromer & Keyes

Marriage, Stevens

Meeting Jesus, Sire

Moneywise, Larsen

One Body, One Spirit, Larsen

Relationships, Hunt

Satisfying Work, Stevens & Schoberg

Senior Saints, Reapsome

The Parables of Jesus, Hunt

When Servants Suffer, Rhodes

BIBLE BOOK STUDIES

Genesis, Fromer & Keyes

Psalms, Klug

Proverbs & Parables, Brestin

Ecclesiastes, Brestin

Jonah, Habakkuk, & Malachi, Fromer & Keyes

Matthew, Sibley

Mark, Christensen

Luke, Keyes

John: Living Word, Kuniholm

Acts 1-12, Christensen

Paul (Acts 13-28), Christensen

Romans: Christian Story (basic), Reapsome

Romans: Made Righteous (advanced), Hunt

1 Corinthians, Hummel

Strengthened to Serve (2 Corinthians), Plueddemann

Galatians, Titus & Philemon, Kuniholm

Ephesians, Baylis

Philippians, Klug

Colossians, Shaw

Letters to the Thessalonians, Fromer & Keyes

Letters to Timothy, Fromer & Keyes

Hebrews, Hunt

James, Christensen

1 & 2 Peter, Jude, Brestin

How Should a Christian Live? (1, 2 & 3 John), Brestin

Revelation, Hunt

BIBLE CHARACTER STUDIES

Ruth & Daniel, Stokes

David: Volume 1, Castleman

David: Volume 2, Castleman

Elijah, Castleman

Job, Klug

Men Like Us, Heidebrecht & Scheuermann

Peter, Castleman

Paul (Acts 13-28), Christensen

Great People of the Bible, Plueddemann

Women Like Us, Barton

Women Who Achieved for God, Christensen

Women Who Believed God, Christensen

Printed in the United States
by Baker & Taylor Publisher Services